H is for Home

written & illustrated by
ROBIN MADERICH

H is for Home

Text and illustrations Copyright Robin Maderich 2020

ISBN: 978-1-7345419-0-8

All rights reserved. No part of this book may be reproduced in any form or by any electronic, digital or mechanical means, including storage and retrieval systems, without written permission of the author, except by a reviewer, who may quote brief passages in a review.

Printed in the United States of America

Potter Street Books

Published by Potter Street Books
www.potterstreetbooks.com

for all inquiries, please see the website contact page

to learn more about the author and her other works, please visit her website: robinmaderichwrites.com

This book is a work designed for enjoyment and sharing. As with any craft project, including those mentioned within, take common sense precautions with items you use during the crafting process, and always assure proper adult supervision.

ABOUT THIS BOOK

H is for Home is a book intended for all ages, from the very young to those who have seen many Christmases but remain, ever and always, young-at-heart.

First and foremost a holiday Alphabet Book, *H is for Home* is meant to be read to those who do not yet read, or even those who do, but still enjoy being read to while snug on a lap or in their beds. Each page contains at least one illustration beginning with that page's letter, so part of the fun is in finding the rest.

This book is also presented for the enjoyment of the family in its entirety. Questions designed to prompt conversation are asked and adult-and-child projects are suggested, but mostly, *H is for Home* is meant to remind us of the joy to be found at this, the most wonderful time of the year, by young and old alike.

This book is dedicated to the child in all of us

At Christmastime, angels on the tree and around the house are symbols of peace and goodwill. Some trees may have glass steeples at the top or stars.

Does your family put up a Christmas tree? Do you help decorate it? What special decoration goes on the top?

What is this angel wearing over her dress? (Hint: it starts with the letter "A")

The first Teddy Bear is believed to have been made by a toymaker in New York City in the early twentieth century. What stuffed animals do you have?
What do you see here?

C is for candy canes, Christmas and cheer; for coziness and comfort and carols we hear.

Christmas means something different to each person. How do you celebrate the season? What do you enjoy the most?

Do you put up a tree? What decorations are special to you? Do you make anything to hang on the branches? Strings of popcorn or paper chains are fun.

Make a simple sock doll like the one sipping tea with his friends (below). Using an old, clean tube sock, stuff the toe with clean rags or a styrofoam ball. Tie brightly colored yarn below the ball for the neck. Make a bow with the yarn. Stuff the rest of the sock with more clean rags and leave an inch or two unstuffed at the bottom. Tie the bottom of the sock with more yarn. Use yarn or pipe cleaners for the arms. Glue or sew them in place. Take a magic marker and make dots for the eyes and a line for the mouth. And you're finished! You can add things like clothes or hair with yarn or the marker. Now you have an extra guest for tea.

E is for EVERGREEN

An evergreen in the snow is a beautiful sight. In the early 1800s, Ernst Anschutz wrote a song called *O Tannebaum* to celebrate his love of the evergreens. This is the first verse of the lovely song we still sing.

O Christmas Tree, O Christmas Tree,
Your branches green delight us.
They're green when summer days are bright;
They're green when winter snow is white.
O Christmas Tree, O Christmas Tree,
Your branches green delight us.

Frosty's Favorite Hot Cocoa
(For Mom or Dad to Make)

Prepare your hot chocolate mix with milk instead of water. Heat the milk and cocoa until hot, but not scalded. In the bottom of each mug to be used place an 1/8 teaspoon of vanilla extract. Pour in the heated cocoa, leaving about an inch of space at the top of each mug. Add a tablespoon of vanilla ice cream to each mug. Top that off with a small mound of whipped cream. Sprinkle a little of the dry cocoa mix onto the whipped cream, and a small amount (just a pinch) of ground cinnamon. Enjoy! (The chocolate should cool enough to drink fairly quickly due to the ice cream, but do check to be sure.)

Of course, do not make if you, your children, or anyone is allergic to any of the ingredients.

Ginger cookies with icing, gingerbread people, gingerbread houses are all great treats during the holidays. Baking as a family is fun. Gingerbread houses can be decorated with gumdrops, hard candies, and icing to hold it all together. Best of all, you can gobble down your house when you finish it, or give it as a gift to someone else.

Why do we give gifts during the holidays? What else do we celebrate? What might you wish for as a gift? What would you like to give?

I is for ICICLE

Icicles form when dripping water freezes. Do you see icicles where you live? If not, why not?

Some places are warm in the winter, others have snow. What is winter like where you live?

Do you know what these are?

J is for Jack-in-the-Box

Is it for you?

Parents: Tell your child about your favorite toy when you were growing up. Did you receive it as a gift for Christmas? If not, when? Who gave it to you? Did you ever have a Jack-in-the-Box? What character jumped out? What music did it play?

Sharing memories with our children and other family members is one of the most special gifts we can give. Your children might surprise you with some favorites of their own!

K is for KINDNESS

L is for LIGHTS

It is believed that Martin Luther was the first person to put lights on a Christmas tree, after seeing the beauty of the stars through the branches of an evergreen tree in the night. In his time, candles were attached to the branches, but today we use strings of electric bulbs made for that purpose.

Does your family hang lights at Christmas? Are they brightly colored or clear?

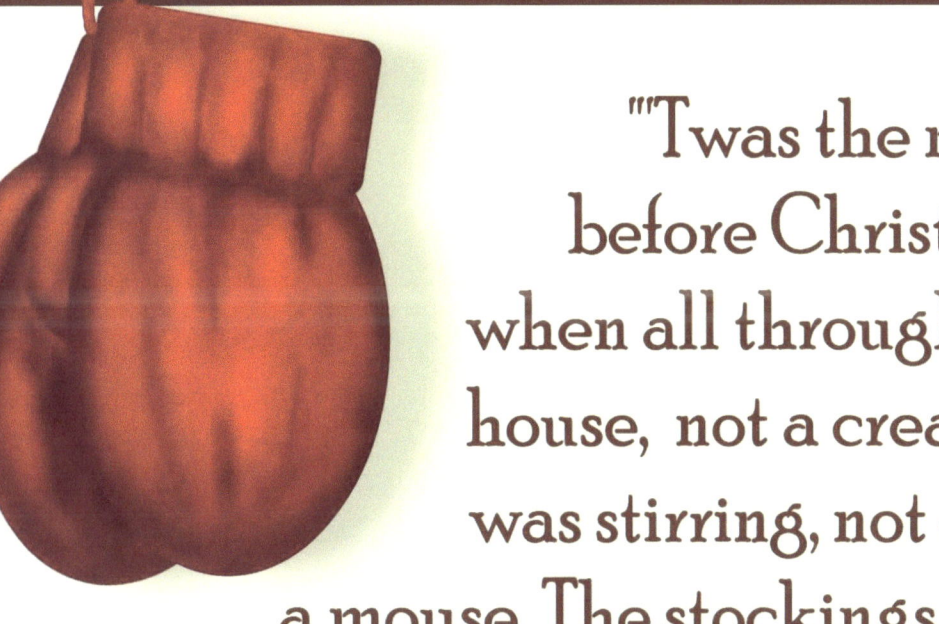

"'Twas the night before Christmas, when all through the house, not a creature was stirring, not even a mouse. The stockings were hung by the chimney with care, in hopes that St. Nicholas soon would be there..."

from *A Visit from St. Nicholas* by Clement Clarke Moore

Take a little time before bed at night to listen to the sounds around you. How are they different from those you hear during the day?

What is different between the sounds of Spring and Winter? Summer and Autumn?

What is your favorite sound at Christmas?

Do you like the music? Bells ringing?

The quiet when snow falls?

The voices of relatives, neighbors and friends who come to visit?

You can decorate a Christmas tree with glass balls or figures, but it is also great fun to make your own ornaments. You can use pipe cleaners, paper mache, ribbon, popcorn and cranberries. You might try cutting last year's holiday cards into shapes and hanging the cutouts from the branches with ribbon. Use your imagination and have fun!

Q is for QUIET

snow softly falling

Make Your Own Paper SNOWFLAKES

Cut a piece of paper into a square. Fold the square top to bottom and then left to right. Holding the paper with the open edges to the right and bottom, start at the lower left-hand corner and round the paper with your safety scissors up to the top right corner. Without opening your folded paper, fold it again so the bottom left and right top corner meet. Cut triangles in the rounded edge. Fold the paper in half long way and cut triangles in the straight edges.
Unfold your paper and you should have a snowflake! You can hang your paper snowflakes with yarn or thread from your tree, a wreath or at the window.

Did you know no two snowflakes are ever alike?

R is for Reindeer

The moon on the breast of the new-fallen snow
Gave the lustre of mid-day to objects below.
When, what to my wondering eyes should appear,
But a miniature sleigh, and eight tiny reindeer.
With a little old driver, so lively and quick,
I knew in a moment it must be St. Nick.
More rapid than eagles his coursers they came,
And he whistled, and shouted, and called them by name. "Now, Dasher! now, Dancer! now, Prancer and Vixen! On, Comet! on, Cupid! on, Donner and Blitzen! To the top of the roof! To the top of the wall! Now dash away, dash away, dash away all!"

from
A Visit from St. Nicholas
by Clement Clarke Moore

S is for Snowglobe

Snowglobes come in many sizes. They have snowmen inside, or Santas, little towns, nativities, and so many other things. When you shake them, the snow swirls over the scene and then settles so you can start it all again.

T is for TOYS

Where is:
The xylophone?
The rocking horse? The yo-yo?
The duck? The jack-in-the-box?
What else do you see?
What might be in the toy box?

Make your own wrapping paper with your kids

Purchase a roll of kraft paper, usually available where you might buy packing supplies. Cut and roll out one length at a time on your table, on top of newspaper to protect the surface.

Cut out shapes from cardstock or index cards. Trace around the shapes on the kraft paper using colored markers and fill them in with other traced shapes, glue dots of colored cardstock from a hole punch, or color completely with crayons, markers or acrylic paints.

You could also use ink pads with glittery colors and stamping blocks from the store. You might apply fingerpaints to your child's hands and have them press the pattern of small hands all over the paper.

Allow everything to dry before wrapping gifts.

Do you have a favorite song?

What holiday song to you like best?

Have you ever been caroling?

What do you think the cat and mouse might be singing?

W is for Wreath

A Family Project

Wreaths prepared from evergreen branches in Winter symbolize the circle of life. A fun family project is to make your own wreath for the front door at Christmastime to welcome visitors to your home. Adults, buy or make a plain wreath, and then you and the youngsters can add elements from nature, using florist wire, yarn or hot glue to attach them to the wreath.

Go outside and look around in the yard. You may find acorns, leaves and pine cones. Perhaps you have dried flowers or can gather seed heads. Queen Anne's Lace (a wildflower) is pretty on wreaths. You could also use slices of dried fruit.

There are other evergreen plants from which you might take clippings. Use your imagination and decorate your wreath in your own celebration of life. Some of the items you use may invite small birds to feast in winter. This is a wonderful way to share your bounty with nature!

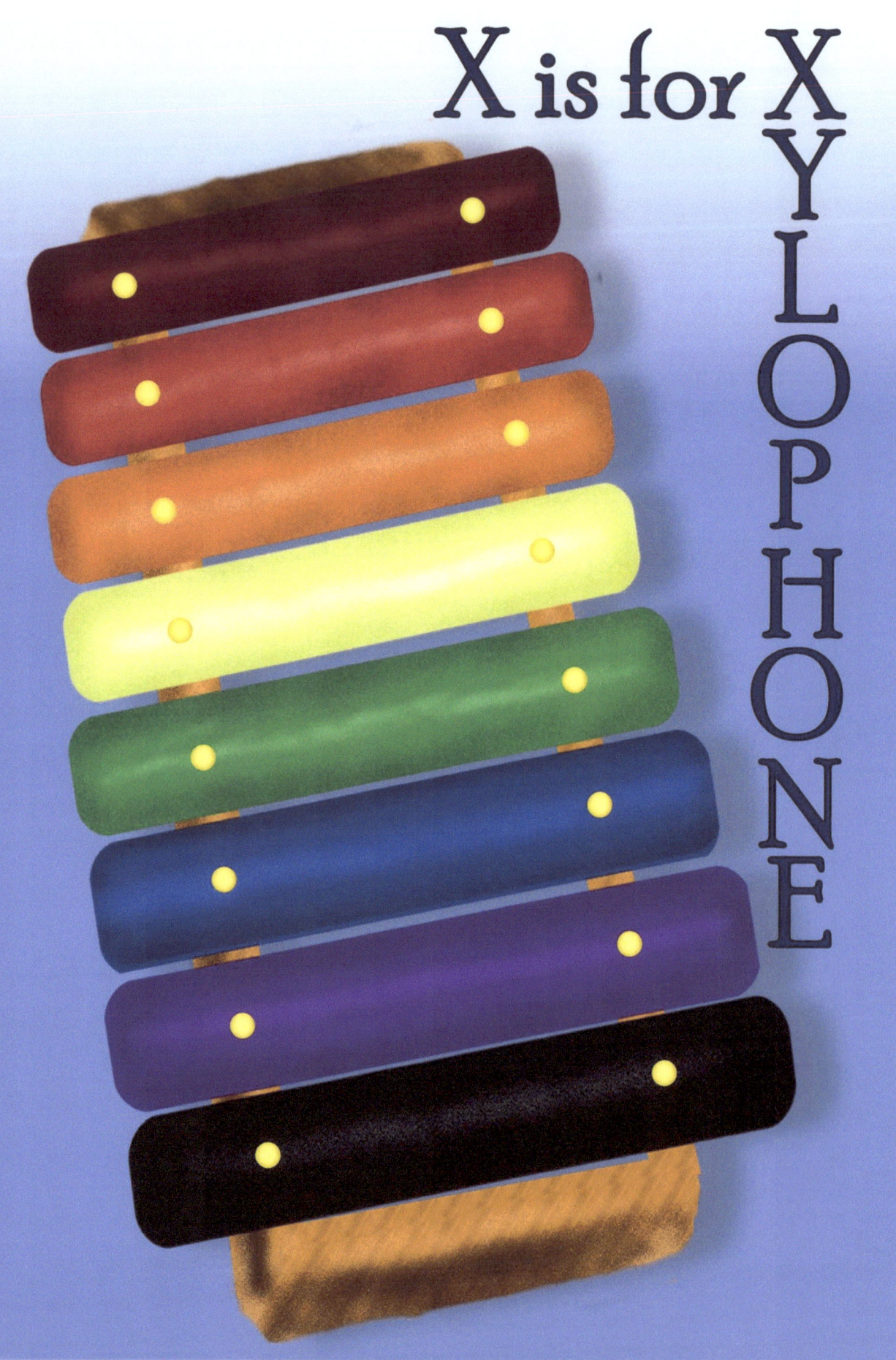

A Xylophone is a musical instrument. When struck, each bar makes a different sound. Toy xylophones are made of wood and metal. They come with sheet music to show you how to play songs by striking the different colored bars in a certain order with special sticks called mallets.

You might even learn some Christmas songs to play for your friends and family. Wouldn't that be fun?

Y is for YUMMY
(cookies for Santa)

Adults: Make your favorite sugar cookie recipe for rolled cookies. Have the kids and like-minded grown-ups cut out shapes with cookie cutters. After baking, see how much fun you can all have decorating your cookies with colored sugar, sprinkles and icing. Package some of the cookies in a tin as a special, homemade gift to a neighbor from your family.

Yum!

Merry Christmas

Just in case you missed one...

A is for Angel, Apple, Apron, Acorn
B is for Bear, Bow, Bunny, Blue Blanket, Block
C is for Christmas, Candy Canes, Candles, Chairs, Cookies, Cushion, Curtains, Cat
D is for Doll, Duck, Dishes, Dog, Dalmation
E is for Evergreen
F is for Friends, Frosty, Furry Feline
G is for Gingerbread (cookie, house, man), Gumdrops, Gifts
H is for Home, House, Hats, Hearts, Holding Hands
I is for Icicles, Ice, Ice skates
J is for Jack-in-the-Box, Joy, Jingle bells
K is for Kindness, Kitten, Kangaroo
L is for Lights
M is for Mantel, Mouse, Mice, Mittens
N is for Night, New moon
O is for Ornaments, Owl
P is for Patridge, Pears, Poinsettia, Puppy, Purple collar
Q is for Quiet
R is for Reindeer, Rocking horse
S is for Snowglobe, Snowman, Snow, Santa, Sack, Star
T is for Toys, Toy chest
U is for Unwrap
V is for Voices, Violet Violin
W is for Wreath, Welcome sign
X is for Xylophone
Y is for Yummy, Yo-Yo
Z is for Zzzz, Zebra

Lightning Source UK Ltd.
Milton Keynes UK
UKHW050628091020
371275UK00005B/43